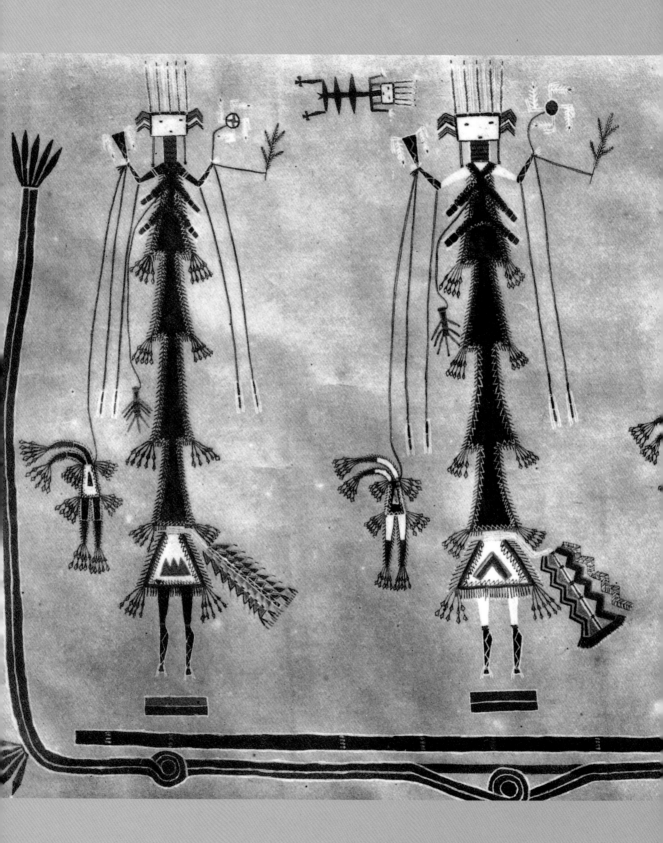

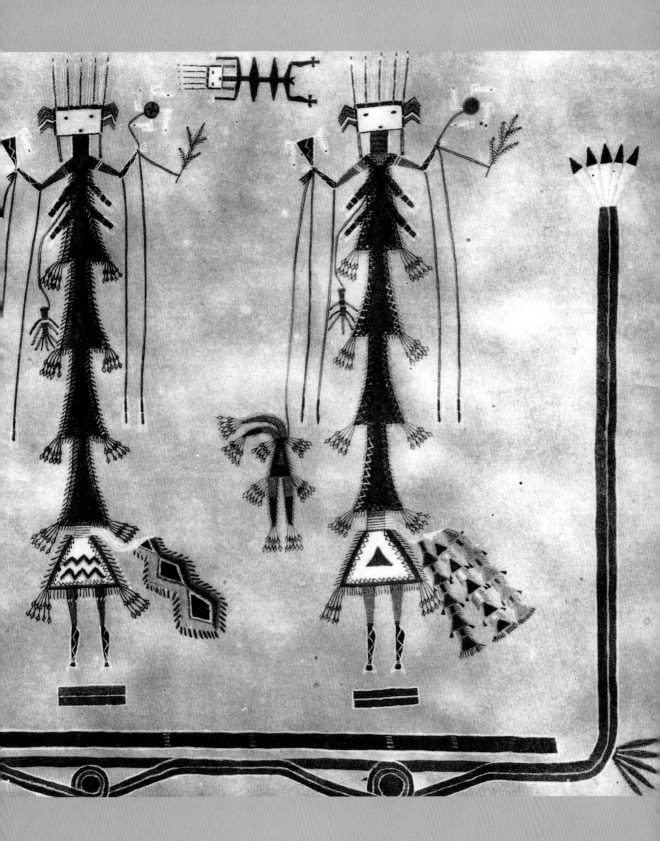

IN A SACRED
MANNER I LIVE

IN A SACRED MANNER I LIVE

Native American Wisdom

Edited by Neil Philip

CLARION BOOKS
NEW YORK

For Elizabeth Law

Clarion Books
a Houghton Mifflin Company imprint
215 Park Avenue South, New York, NY 10003

Published in the United States in 1997 by arrangement with
The Albion Press Ltd., Spring Hill, Idbury, Oxfordshire OX7 6RU, England
Volume copyright © 1997 The Albion Press Ltd.
Selection and introduction copyright © 1997 Neil Philip
Copyright in individual passages and photographs copyright © 1997
as noted specifically in the acknowledgments on pp. 92–93.
First Clarion paperback edition, 2005.

www.houghtonmifflinbooks.com

Library of Congress Cataloging-in-Publication Data

In a sacred manner I live : Native American wisdom / edited by Neil Philip.
p.   cm.
Includes bibliographical references.
Summary: A collection of speeches, or portions of speeches, made by Native Americans.
ISBN: 0-395-84981-0
1. Speeches, addresses, etc., Indian—North America—Juvenile
literature. 2. Indian philosophy—North America—Juvenile
literature. 3. Human ecology—North America—Philosophy—Juvenile
literature. [1. Indian philosophy—North America. 2. Indians of
North America.] I. Philip, Neil.
E98.O7 S33 1997
970'.00497—dc21   96006509
CIP
AC

CL ISBN–13: 978-0-395-84981-1   CL ISBN–10: 0-395-84981-0
PA ISBN–13: 978-0-618-60483-8   PA ISBN–10: 0-618-60483-9

Typesetting by York House Typographic, London
Duotone origination by York House Graphics, London
Printed in China by South China Printing Company

10 9 8 7 6 5 4 3 2

ENDPAPERS: Edward S. Curtis *Mountain Chant sand-painting* Navajo 1907
HALF-TITLE: Edward S. Curtis *A mountain camp* Yakima 1910 (detail)
FACING TITLE PAGE: James Mooney Tewa 1892–3 (detail)

INTRODUCTION

The speakers and writers in this book range from Chief Powhatan, in 1609, to the contemporary Sioux medicine man Leonard Crow Dog in 1995. This time span begins when Native American cultures still reigned supreme across North America from Massachusetts to California, and takes us through years of heartbreak, treachery, and cultural breakdown to the present day, when traditional Native American values and beliefs are once again resurgent, both among Native Americans and in the world at large.

Despite the huge differences between, say, Plains and Pueblo Indians, it is possible to speak of "Native American wisdom" and mean something fairly specific. That meaning is summed up in this book's title, *In a Sacred Manner I Live*. To live in a sacred manner is to live with respect for the environment, for the community, and for oneself. It is a way of looking at life that was shared by all the Indian nations.

Native American culture was not, like that of the whites, based on change and progress, but on harmony and tradition. The collision between two such world views, when one party was so much stronger than the other, led to misunderstanding and tragedy. But the Native American way did not, as expected, die out. And today, in a written culture and a changed world, young Native Americans are reclaiming their heritage.

Part of that heritage, which can be seen in the work of many Native American writers, is a profound respect for the power of language. This respect, which brings with it a wonderful economy, directness, and precision, is based on the weight which Native Americans attached to the spoken word. The heartfelt eloquence of Native American oratory — which so astonished and bemused white negotiators at treaty talks — arose from a culture in which a word, once spoken, never died.

Edward S. Curtis *In a Piegan lodge*
Piegan 1910. The men are Little
Plume and his son, Yellow Kidney.

The Pulitzer Prize–winning Kiowa author N. Scott Momaday writes in *The Way to Rainy Mountain* (University of New Mexico Press, 1969), "A word has power in and of itself. It comes from nothing into sound and meaning. It gives origin to all things. By means of words can a man deal with the world on equal terms. And the word is sacred."

The words in this book were recorded in various ways. Almost all have been translated from the original language of the Indian speaker, and — while I have striven to use the most authentic sources — the earlier the date, the less we can be sure that the translation is true to what was said. The most obvious case is that of the renowned orator Chief Seattle. His famous speech to Governor Isaac Stevens in 1854 was not written down until over twenty years later, when Dr. Henry A. Smith, who had heard the speech, published it in the *Seattle Sunday Star* of October 29, 1877. Nevertheless, Seattle's words, even couched in Dr. Smith's voice, retain that sacred power to move us to tears.

The rather formal wording of nineteenth-century translators does mask one important aspect of Native American wisdom: its humor. To live in a sacred manner is not to live in solemn self-denial, but to take pleasure in being alive in the world. The last line of a Wintu prayer from California sums it up:

Today, I shall be happy.

NEIL PHILIP

Edward S. Curtis *The Hunka Alowanpi Ceremony* Oglala Sioux 1907. This is known as the relation-making ceremony, because it creates a deep unbreakable bond between two people. The hairs dangling from the sticks are horse-tails, and represent the White Buffalo Calf Maiden, whose holy pipe is consecrated over a painted buffalo skull altar lying on a bed of sweet sage.

IN A SACRED MANNER I LIVE

In a sacred manner
I live
to the heavens
I gazed
in a sacred manner
I live
my horses
are many

Bear Eagle *Mato-wanbli*

TETON SIOUX *Lakota*

Bear Eagle learned this song from
Shell Necklace, *Panke-ska-napin.* It is
one of over 200 songs recorded at
Standing Rock Reservation between
1911 and 1914 by Frances Densmore
and her Sioux interpreter and
assistant, Robert P. Higheagle.

14

LOOKING INTO THE FUTURE

You look at me, and you see only an ugly old man, but within I am filled with great beauty. I sit as on a mountaintop and I look into the future. I see my people and your people living together. In time to come my people will have forgotten their early way of life unless they learn it from white men's books. So you must write down all that I will tell you; and you must have it made into a book that coming generations may know this truth.

Old Man Buffalo Grass *Sandoval, Hastin Tlotsi hee*

NAVAJO *Diné*

Old Man Buffalo Grass, first of the four chiefs of the Navajo, told Aileen O'Bryan the myths of his people over seventeen days in late 1928, his nephew Sam Ahkeah acting as interpreter. He died the following January.

Edward S. Curtis *Nesjaja Hatali* Navajo 1904. The sitter was a well-known medicine man. He made the Mountain Chant sand-painting featured on this book's endpapers

BEHOLD THIS DAY

And a Voice said: "All over the universe they have finished a day of happiness." And looking down I saw that the whole wide circle of the day was beautiful and green, with all fruits growing and all things kind and happy.

Then a Voice said: "Behold this day, for it is yours to make. Now you shall stand upon the center of the earth to see, for there they are taking you."

I was still on my bay horse, and once more I felt the riders of the west, the north, the east, the south, behind me in formation, as before, and we were going east. I looked ahead and saw the mountains there with rocks and forests on them, and from the mountains flashed all colors upward to the heavens. Then I was standing on the highest mountain of them all, and round about beneath me was the whole hoop of the world. And while I stood there I saw more than I can tell and I understood more than I saw; for I was seeing in a sacred manner the shapes of all things in the spirit, and the shape of all shapes as they must live together like one being. And I saw that the sacred hoop of my people was one of many hoops that made one circle, wide as daylight and as starlight, and in the center grew one mighty flowering tree to shelter all the children of one mother and one father. And I saw that it was holy.

Black Elk *Hehaka Sapa*

OGLALA SIOUX *Lakota*

John C. H. Grabill *Brulé village near Pine Ridge, South Dakota* Brulé Sioux 1891. This photograph, taken shortly after the massacre at Wounded Knee, represents the calm after the storm.

Black Elk (1863–1950), a holy man of the Oglala Sioux, told the story of his life and his vision to the poet John G. Neihardt in 1931. He received the great vision by which he steered his life at the age of nine.

Laura Gilpin *Sand painting at a Yeibichai Ceremony* Navajo 1951. Taken at a Nightway ceremony near Shiprock, New Mexico.

The Yeibichai ceremony, or Nightway Chant, is one of the most sacred and important of the Navajo rites. It lasts for nine nights, and its primary purpose is healing. The fragment opposite was obtained from Hatali Natloi and translated by Washington Matthews, a white surgeon who studied the Nightway between 1880 and 1902, when he published his classic book *The Night Chant*.

IN BEAUTY MAY I WALK

In beauty may I walk.
All day long may I walk.
Through the returning seasons may I walk. . . .
On the trail marked with pollen may I walk.
With grasshoppers about my feet may I walk.
With dew about my feet may I walk.
With beauty may I walk.
With beauty before me, may I walk.
With beauty behind me, may I walk.
With beauty above me, may I walk.
With beauty below me, may I walk.
With beauty all around me, may I walk.
In old age wandering on a trail of beauty,
Lively, may I walk.
In old age wandering on a trail of beauty,
Living again, may I walk.
It is finished in beauty.
It is finished in beauty.

from the Nightway Chant

NAVAJO *Diné*

THE SPRING

Behold, my brothers, the spring has come; the earth has received the embraces of the sun and we shall soon see the results of that love!

Every seed is awakened and so has all animal life. It is through this mysterious power that we too have our being and we therefore yield to our neighbors, even our animal neighbors, the same right as ourselves, to inhabit this land.

Sitting Bull *Tatanka Yotanka*

HUNKPAPA SIOUX *Lakota*

Sitting Bull, war chief and holy man of the Hunkpapa Sioux, was born in 1831 and assassinated on December 15, 1890. He made this speech at a Powder River council in 1877.

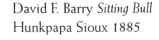

David F. Barry *Sitting Bull* Hunkpapa Sioux 1885

THE SUN GOD

We believe that the Sun God is all powerful, for every spring he makes the trees to bud and the grass to grow. We see these things with our own eyes, and therefore know that all life comes from him.

Anonymous

BLACKFOOT *Siksika*

The whites could not understand the deep spirituality of the Sun Dance of the Plains Indians, in which warriors underwent self-torture to strengthen their prayers. When this man spoke in 1910, the Sun Dance had been banned for a generation. Restrictions were lifted in the 1930s, and today there has been a revival of the old traditions.

Edward S. Curtis *Sun dancer*
Sioux 1907

THE SUN AND THE EARTH

All living creatures and all plants derive their life from the sun. If it were not for the sun, there would be darkness and nothing could grow — the earth would be without life. Yet the sun must have the help of the earth. If the sun alone were to act upon animals and plants, the heat would be so great that they would die, but there are clouds that bring rain, and the action of the sun and earth together supplies the moisture that is needed for life. The roots of a plant go down, and the deeper they go the more moisture they find. This is according to the laws of nature and is one of the evidences of the wisdom of Wakan Tanka. Plants are sent by Wakan Tanka and come from the ground at his command, the part to be affected by the sun and rain appearing above the ground and the roots pressing downward to find the moisture which is supplied for them. Animals and plants are taught by Wakan Tanka what they are to do. Wakan Tanka teaches the birds to make nests, yet the nests of all birds are not alike. Wakan Tanka gives them merely the outline. Some make better nests than others.

Shooter *Okute*

TETON SIOUX *Lakota*

Shooter, "a thoughtful man and well versed in the old customs," was speaking to a fellow Sioux, Robert P. Higheagle. Wakan Tanka translates as Great Mystery or Great Spirit.

Walter McClintock *A horse race* Blackfoot 1906

THE EARTH

The earth is your grandmother and mother, and she is
sacred. Every step that is taken upon her should be as
a prayer.

Black Elk *Hehaka Sapa*

OGLALA SIOUX *Lakota*

According to Black Elk, these words
were spoken by *Ptesan Win*, White
Buffalo Calf Woman, when she
brought the sacred pipe to the Sioux.
In 1947–8, Black Elk passed on his
knowledge of the sacred rites of the
Sioux to Joseph Epes Brown.
He died in 1950.

THE EARTH IS OUR MOTHER

A long time ago the earth was placed here for us, the people, the Navajo; it gives us corn and we consider her our mother.

. . . The Earth is our mother. The white man is ruining our mother. I don't know the white man's ways but to us the Mesa, the air, the water, are Holy Elements. We pray to these Holy Elements in order for our people to flourish and perpetuate the well-being of each generation.

Even when we are small, our cradle is made from the things given to us from Mother Earth. We use these elements all of our lives and when we die we go back to Mother Earth.

When we were first put on earth, the herbs and medicine were also put here for us to use. These have become part of our prayers to Mother Earth. We should realize it for if we forget these things we will vanish as the people. That is why I don't like the coal mine.

Asa Bazhonoodah

NAVAJO *Diné*

Asa Bazhonoodah, a Navajo born at Black Mesa in 1888, gave this speech in Washington during Senate hearings on open-pit mining on Black Mesa in spring 1971.

Laura Gilpin *Navajo woman, child, and lambs* Navajo 1931

Anita Alvarez de Williams *Adelaida*
telling her dream Cocopa 1972

26

THE SPIRIT OF THE EARTH

The white people never cared for land or deer
or bear. When we Indians kill meat, we eat it all up.
When we dig roots, we make little holes. When we
build houses, we make little holes. When we burn
grass for grasshoppers, we don't ruin things. We shake
down acorns and pinenuts. We don't chop down the
trees. We only use dead wood. But the white people
plow up the ground, pull up the trees, kill everything.
The tree says, "Don't. I am sore. Don't hurt me." But
they chop it down and cut it up. The spirit of the land
hates them. They blast out trees and stir it up to its
depths. They saw up the trees. That hurts them. The
Indians never hurt anything, but the white people
destroy all. They blast rocks and scatter them on the
earth. The rock says, "Don't. You are hurting me." But
the white people pay no attention. When the Indians
use rocks, they take little round ones for their
cooking. The white people dig deep long tunnels.
They make roads. They dig as much as they wish.
They don't care how much the ground cries out. How
can the spirit of the earth like the white man? . . .
Everywhere the white man has touched it, it is
sore.

Kate Luckie

WINTU

Kate Luckie was a powerful shaman
of the Wintu of California.
She spoke these words in 1925.

YOU ASK ME TO PLOW THE GROUND!

You ask me to plow the ground! Shall I take a knife
and tear my mother's bosom? Then when I die she will
not take me to her bosom to rest.

   You ask me to dig for stone! Shall I dig under her
skin for her bones? Then when I die I cannot enter her
body to be born again.

   You ask me to cut grass and make hay and sell it,
and be rich like white men! But how dare I cut off my
mother's hair!

Smohalla

WANAPAM *Columbia River Indians*

Smohalla's Dreamer religion
foreshadowed the Ghost Dance.
He was born between 1815 and 1820
and began preaching around 1850.
Chief Joseph of the Nez Percé was
greatly influenced by his teachings.

Benjamin Gifford *Indians overlooking the*
falls of the Columbia River, Celilo, Oregon
Columbia River Indians c.1899

OVERLEAF: Edward S. Curtis *At the water's edge* Piegan 1910

LAND CANNOT BE SOLD

My reason teaches me that *land cannot be sold.* The Great Spirit gave it to his children to live upon, and cultivate as far as is necessary for their subsistence; and so long as they occupy and cultivate it, they have the right to the soil — but if they voluntarily leave it, then any other people have a right to settle upon it. Nothing can be sold but such things as can be carried away.

Black Hawk *Makataimeshekiakiak*

SAUK

Black Hawk, chief of the Sauk and Fox Indians, was their leader in the Black Hawk War of 1832. He dictated an account of his life the following year, through the interpreter Antoine Leclair.

LAND IS MORE VALUABLE THAN MONEY

Our land is more valuable than your money. It will last forever. It will not even perish by the flames of fire. As long as the sun shines and the waters flow, this land will be here to give life to men and animals. We cannot sell the lives of men and animals. It was put here for us by the Great Spirit and we cannot sell it because it does not belong to us. You can count your money and burn it within the nod of a buffalo's head, but only the Great Spirit can count the grains of sand and the blades of grass on the plains. As a present to you, we will give you anything we have that you can take with you; but the land, never.

Crowfoot

BLACKFOOT Siksika

1877

THE TRUE TEACHER

For a great many years [my people] have listened to your teachings. These people's fathers were not without instruction. The earth was their teacher. That is the true teacher. That is where the Indian first discovered that he was a human being. Our forefathers taught their successors that were left on the earth. In the same way, from the earth, your fathers spring, and the earth taught you in the same way. . . . When they hunted for happiness, they searched the ground first.

Homli

WALLAWALLA

1870–1

Edward S. Curtis *Piopio-maksmaks* Wallawalla 1905. This is the son of the Piopio-maksmaks who in 1855 as principal chief of the Wallawalla negotiated a treaty with Governor Isaac Stevens.

THE INDIAN COUNTRY

God created this Indian country and it was like
he spread out a big blanket. He put the Indians on it.
They were created here in this country, truly and
honestly, and that was the time this river started to
run. Then God created fish in this river and put deer
in these mountains and made laws through which has
come the increase of fish and game. Then the Creator
gave us Indians life; we awakened and as soon as we
saw the game and fish we knew that they were made
for us. For the women God made roots and berries to
gather, and the Indians grew and multiplied as a
people. When we were created we were given our
ground to live on, and from that time these were our
rights. This is all true. We had the fish before the
missionaries came, before the white man came. We
were put here by the Creator and these were our
rights as far as my memory to my great-grandfather.
This was the food on which we lived. My mother
gathered berries; my father fished and killed the game.
These words are mine and they are true. It matters not
how long I live, I cannot change these thoughts. My
strength is from the fish; my blood is from the fish,
from the roots and the berries. The fish and the game
are the essence of my life. I was not brought from a
foreign country and did not come here. I was put here
by the Creator.

George Meninock

YAKIMA

1915   Edward S. Curtis *The Fisherman* Wishram 1909

A STAR WHISPER

I had a vision. It came from the morning star, a star
whisper. I heard this voice saying, "Any understanding
you ask from the morning star shall be granted you,
but ask with the sacred things, the drum, the sacred
tobacco, the sacred sweet grass, and, above all, with
the sacred pipe." Our dead sleep not. They tell me
what I want to know. I have the power to see through
things. I have only limited vision with the eyes I have
in my head, but with my spiritual eyes I can see across
oceans. The pipe is here to unite us, to remove the
fences people put up against one another. Putting up
fences is the white man's way. He invented the barbed
wire, the barbed wire of the heart. The pipe is a fence
remover. Sitting in a circle, smoking it the right way,
all barriers disappear. Walls crumble.

Leonard Crow Dog *Kangi Shunka Manitou*

BRULÉ SIOUX *Lakota*

Leonard Crow Dog, born in 1942, is
spiritual leader of AIM, the American
Indian Movement. He published his
family autobiography in 1995, in
collaboration with the writer Richard
Erdoes.

Edward S. Curtis *A sacred pipe* Piegan 1910

THE GREAT CIRCLE

You have noticed that everything an Indian does is in a circle, and that is because the Power of the World always works in circles, and everything tries to be round. In the old days when we were a strong and happy people, all our power came to us from the sacred hoop of the nation, and so long as the hoop was unbroken, the people flourished. The flowering tree was the living center of the hoop, and the circle of the four quarters nourished it. The east gave peace and light, the south gave warmth, the west gave rain, and the north with its cold and mighty wind gave strength and endurance. This knowledge came to us from the outer world with our religion. Everything the Power of the World does is done in a circle. The sky is round, and I have heard that the earth is round like a ball, and so are all the stars. The wind, in its greatest power, whirls. Birds make their nests in circles, for theirs is the same religion as ours. The sun comes forth and goes down again in a circle. The moon does the same, and both are round.

Even the seasons form a great circle in their changing, and always come back again to where they were. The life of a man is a circle from childhood to childhood, and so it is in everything where power moves. Our tipis were round like the nests of birds, and these were always set in a circle, the nation's hoop, a nest of many nests, where the Great Spirit meant for us to hatch our children.

Black Elk *Hehaka Sapa*
OGLALA SIOUX *Lakota* 1931

Joseph Epes Brown *Black Elk* Oglala Sioux 1947

Frank Fiske *The tipi of Chief Old Bull* Hunkpapa Sioux c.1900

THE TIPI

The tipi is much better to live in; always clean, warm
in winter, cool in summer; easy to move. The white
man builds big house, cost much money, like big cage,
shut out sun, can never move; always sick. Indians and
animals know better how to live than white man;
nobody can be in good health if he does not have all
the time fresh air, sunshine, and good water. If the
Great Spirit wanted men to stay in one place he would
make the world stand still; but he made it to always
change, so birds and animals can move and always
have green grass and ripe berries, sunlight to work and
play, and night to sleep; summer for flowers to bloom,
and winter for them to sleep; always changing;
everything for good; nothing for nothing.

Flying Hawk

OGLALA SIOUX *Lakota*

Flying Hawk (1852–1931) was a
nephew of Sitting Bull. His Indian's-
eye view of U.S. history, *Firewater and
Forked Tongues*, recorded and edited by
M. I. McCreight, was published in
1947.

THIS I BELIEVE

Our fathers gave us many laws, which they had learned from their fathers. These laws were good. They told us to treat all men as they treated us; that we should never be the first to break a bargain; that it was a disgrace to tell a lie; that we should speak only the truth; that it was a shame for one man to take from another his wife or his property without paying for it. We were taught to believe that the Great Spirit sees and hears everything, and that he never forgets; that hereafter he will give every man a spirit-home according to his deserts: if he has been a good man, he will have a good home; if he has been a bad man, he will have a bad home. This I believe, and all my people believe the same.

Chief Joseph *Inmutooyahlatlat*

NEZ PERCÉ *Tsutpeli*

Chief Joseph, who had led the previously peaceable Nez Percés on the warpath two years earlier, was invited to address Congress on January 14, 1879, to put his case.

De Lancey Gill *Chief Joseph* Nez Percé 1903. Chief Joseph was a man of peace, proud of the fact that up until 1877 no Nez Percé had killed a white man; but his skills as a general were compared with those of Xenophon and Napoleon.

John Alvin Anderson *Sam Kills Two painting a winter count* Brulé Sioux 1910

44

A POWER GREATER THAN MAN

When a man does a piece of work which is admired
by all we say that it is wonderful; but when we see the
changes of day and night, the sun, moon, and stars in
the sky, and the changing seasons upon the earth,
with their ripening fruits, anyone must realize that it is
the work of some one more powerful than man.
Greatest of all is the sun, without which we could not
live. The birds and the beasts, the trees and the rocks,
are the work of some great power. Sometimes men say
that they can understand the meaning of the songs of
birds. I can believe this is true. They say that they can
understand the call and cry of the animals, and I can
believe this also is true, for these creatures and man
are alike the work of a great power. We often wish for
things to come, as the rain or the snow. They do not
always come when we wish, but they are sure to come
in time, for they are under the control of a power that
is greater than man.

Chased-by-Bears *Mato-kuwa*

SANTEE-YANKTONAI SIOUX *Lakota*

Chased-by-Bears was one of Frances
Densmore's principal informants on
the Sun Dance, although he told her
"It is so sacred to us that we do not
talk of it often." He was born in 1843
and died in 1915.

THE DUTY OF PRAYER

In the life of the Indian there was only one inevitable
duty — the duty of prayer — the daily recognition of
the Unseen and Eternal. His daily devotions were
more necessary to him than daily food. He wakes at
daybreak, puts on his moccasins, and steps down to
the water's edge. Here he throws handfuls of clear,
cold water into his face, or plunges in bodily. After
the bath, he stands erect before the advancing dawn,
facing the sun as it dances upon the horizon, and
offers his unspoken orison. His mate may precede or
follow him in his devotions, but never accompanies
him. Each soul must meet the morning sun, the new
sweet earth, and the Great Silence alone!

Whenever, in the course of the daily hunt, the red
hunter comes upon a scene that is strikingly beautiful
or sublime — a black thundercloud with the rainbow's
glowing arch above the mountain, a white waterfall in
the heart of a green gorge; a vast prairie tinged with
the blood-red of sunset — he pauses for an instant in
the attitude of worship. He sees no need for setting
apart one day in seven as a holy day, since to him all
days are God's.

Charles A. Eastman *Ohiyesa*

WAHPETON SIOUX *Lakota*

Charles A. Eastman (1858–1939) was
one of the first Native American
authors to achieve widespread fame.

Edward S. Curtis *Getting water* Apache 1903

Lloyd Winter and Percy Pond *The
Whale House, home of Chief Klart-Reech*
Tlingit 1895

WHEN AN INDIAN PRAYS

When an Indian prays he doesn't read a lot of words
out of a book. He just says a very short prayer. If you
say a long one you won't understand yourself what
you are saying. And so the last thing I can teach you,
if you want to be taught by an old man living in a
dilapidated shack, a man who went to the third grade
for eight years, is this prayer, which I use when I am
crying for a vision:

   "Wakan Tanka, Tunkashila, *onshimala* . . .
Grandfather Spirit, pity me, so that my people may
live."

Lame Deer *Tahca Ushte*

MINICONJOU SIOUX *Lakota*

Lame Deer (also known as John Fire),
a Sioux medicine man, told his life
story to Richard Erdoes in 1972.

THERE WAS A TIME

Brother! Listen to what we say. There was a time when our forefathers owned this great island. Their seats extended from the rising to the setting sun. The Great Spirit had made it for the use of Indians. He had created the buffalo, the deer, and other animals for food. He made the bear and the beaver, and their skins served us for clothing. He had scattered them over the country, and taught us how to take them. He had caused the earth to produce corn for bread. All this he had done for his red children because he loved them. If we had any disputes about hunting-grounds, they were generally settled without the shedding of much blood.

But an evil day came upon us. Your forefathers crossed the great waters, and landed on this island. Their numbers were small. They found friends and not enemies. They told us they had fled from their own country for fear of wicked men, and had come here to enjoy their religion. They asked for a small seat. We took pity on them, granted their request, and they sat down amongst us. We gave them corn and meat. They gave us poison in return. The white people had now found our country.

Tidings were carried back, and more came amongst us. Yet we did not fear them. We took them to be friends. They called us brothers. We believed them, and gave them a larger seat. At length their numbers had greatly increased. They wanted more land. They wanted our country. Our eyes were opened, and our minds became uneasy. Wars took place. Indians were

David Noble *Mohawk steelworker, New York City* Mohawk 1970

hired to fight against Indians, and many of our people
were destroyed. They also brought strong liquor among
us. It was strong and powerful, and has slain thousands.
Brother! Our seats were once large, and yours were
very small. You have now become a great people, and
we have scarcely a place left to spread our blankets.
You have got our country, but are not satisfied. You
want to force your religion upon us.

Red Jacket *Sagoyewatha*

SENECA *Iroquois 1805*

James Mooney *Swimmer, Cherokee medicine man* Cherokee 1888

GET A LITTLE FARTHER

Brothers! We have heard the talk of our great father; it is very kind. He says he loves his red children. Brothers! When the white man first came to these shores, the Muskogees gave him land, and kindled him a fire to make him comfortable; and when the pale faces of the south made war on him, their young men drew the tomahawk, and protected his head from the scalping knife. But when the white man had warmed himself before the Indian's fire, and filled himself with the Indian's hominy, he became very large; he stopped not for the mountaintops, and his feet covered the plains and the valleys. His hands grasped the eastern and the western sea. Then he became our great father. He loved his red children; but said, "You must move a little farther, lest I should, by accident, tread on you." With one foot he pushed the red man over the Oconee, and with the other he trampled down the graves of his fathers. But our great father still loved his red children, and he soon made them another talk. He said much; but it all meant nothing, but "Move a little farther; you are too near me."

. . . Brothers! I have listened to a great many talks from our great father. But they always began and ended in this, "Get a little farther; you are too near me."

I have spoken.

Speckled Snake

CREEK Muskogee

Speckled Snake was over 100 years old when he made this speech in 1830.

WORDS DO NOT PAY

I do not understand why nothing is done for my people. I have heard talk and talk, but nothing is done. Good words do not last long unless they amount to something. Words do not pay for my dead people. They do not pay for my country, now overrun by white men. They do not protect my father's grave. They do not pay for all my horses and cattle. Good words will not give me back my children. Good words will not make good the promise of your war chief General Miles. Good words will not give my people good health and stop them from dying. Good words will not get my people a home where they can live in peace and take care of themselves. I am tired of talk that comes to nothing. It makes my heart sick when I remember all the good words and all the broken promises. There has been too much talking by men who had no right to talk. Too many misrepresentations have been made, too many misunderstandings have come up between the white men about the Indians. If the white man wants to live in peace with the Indian he can live in peace. There need be no trouble. Treat all men alike. Give them all the same law. Give them all an even chance to live and grow. All men were made by the same Great Spirit Chief. They are all brothers. The earth is the mother of all people, and all people should have equal rights upon it. You might as well expect the rivers to run backward as that any man who was born a free man should be contented when penned up and denied liberty to go where he pleases. . . .

54

Fair and Thompson *Ewetonemy, Nez Percé girl* Nez Percé c.1900

Let me be a free man — free to travel, free to stop,
free to work, free to trade where I choose, free to
choose my own teachers, free to follow the religion of
my fathers, free to think and talk and act for myself —
and I will obey every law, or submit to the penalty.

Chief Joseph *Inmutooyahlatlat*

NEZ PERCÉ *Tsutpeli*

Chief Joseph's eloquence fell on deaf ears.
He never saw his homeland again.

IT IS TRUE

It is true I am a Shawnee. My forefathers were warriors. Their son is a warrior. From them I only take my existence; from my tribe I take nothing. I am the maker of my own fortune; and oh! that I could make that of my red people, and of my country, as great as the conceptions of my mind, when I think of the Spirit that rules the universe. I would not then come to Governor Harrison, to ask him to tear the treaty, and to obliterate the landmark; but I would say to him, Sir, you have liberty to return to your own country.

Tecumseh

SHAWNEE

Tecumseh made this protest to Governor William Henry Harrison on August 12, 1810, over the land sales of 1805–6. He refused to enter the Governor's mansion.

Thomas M. Easterly *Longhorn* Sauk and Fox 1846–7

I DO NOT SEE ANY GOOD

I do not see any good that it would do me to put a
bullet through your body — I could not make any use of
you when dead; but I could of a rabbit or turkey. As to
myself, I think it more wise to avoid than to put
myself in the way of harm; I am under apprehension
that you might hit me. That being the case, I think it
advisable to keep my distance. If you want to try your
pistols, take some object — a tree, or anything about my
size; and if you hit that, send me word, and I shall
acknowledge, that had I been there you might have
hit me.

Kahkewaquonaby

OJIBWA *Chippewa*

Kahkewaquonaby (1802–1856) was,
as Rev. Peter Jones, a minister of the
Wesleyan Methodist Church. He
used this position to argue for Indian
rights, as in this anecdote illustrating
the superior "sense" and "moral
courage" of the Indian.

Edward O. Beaman *Ute warrior and boy* Ute 1871 (detail)

60

PEACE AND WAR

I know the difference of peace and war better than
any in my country. But now I am old and before long
must die. . . . What good will it do you to take by force
that which you may have by love, or to destroy
those that provide you with food? What can you get
by war, when we can hide our provisions, and fly to
the woods, so that you must famish by wronging us,
your friends?

    . . . Do you think I am so simple, not to know it is
better to eat good meat, lie well, and sleep quietly
with my women and children, to laugh and be merry
with you, have copper, hatchets, or what I want, being
your friend, than be forced to fly from all, to lie cold
in the woods, feed upon acorns, roots, and such trash;
and so be hunted by you, that I can neither rest, eat,
nor sleep; but my tired men must watch, and if a twig
but break, everyone cries, "Here comes Captain
Smith!"; so I must fly I know not where, and thus in
miserable fear end my miserable life?

    . . . Come in a friendly manner to see us, and not
thus with your guns and swords.

Powhatan *Wahunsonacock*

POWHATAN CONFEDERACY

De Lancey Gill *William Terrill Bradby,*
Pamunkey Indian Pamunkey 1899.
The Pamunkey were part of
the Powhatan Confederacy.

Powhatan was the father of Pocahontas,
who in 1607 begged him to spare the
life of the man to whom these words
were addressed — John Smith.

LOOK AT ME

Look at me, I am poor and naked, but I am the chief of the nation. We do not want riches but we do want to train our children right. Riches would do us no good. We could not take them with us to the other world. We do not want riches, we want peace and love.

Red Cloud *Mahpiua Luta*

OGLALA SIOUX *Lakota*

Red Cloud, principal chief of the Oglala Sioux, was born in 1822. He gave this speech at the Cooper Institute, New York, on January 16, 1870.

Edward S. Curtis *Red Cloud* Oglala Sioux 1905. Red Cloud was both a shrewd negotiator and a master of guerrilla warfare. He refused to attend treaty talks at Fort Laramie until the army abandoned its forts on tribal lands along the Powder River.

Edward S. Curtis *Night scout* Nez Percé 1910

I WANT PEACE

The sun has been very hot on my head and made me
as in a fire; my blood was on fire, but now I have come
into this valley and drunk of these waters and washed
myself in them and they have cooled me. Now that I
am cool I have come with my hands open to you to
live in peace with you. I speak straight and do not
wish to deceive or be deceived. I want a good, strong,
and lasting peace. When God made the world he gave
one part to the white man and another to the Apache.
Why was it? Why did they come together? Now that I
am to speak, the sun, the moon, the earth, the air, the
waters, the birds and beasts, even the children unborn
shall rejoice at my words. The white people have
looked for me long. I am here! What do they want?
They have looked for me long; why am I worth so
much? If I am worth so much why not mark where I set
my foot and look when I spit? The coyotes go about
at night to rob and kill; I cannot see them; I am not
God. I am no longer chief of all the Apaches. I am no
longer rich; I am but a poor man. The world was not
always this way. I cannot command the animals; if I
would they would not obey me. God made us not as
you; we were born like the animals, in the dry grass,
not on beds like you.

Cochise

CHIRICAHUA APACHE *Inde*

Cochise, who died in 1874, spoke these words in 1871.

I WILL FIGHT NO MORE

Tell General Howard I know his heart. What he told me before, I have in my heart.

I am tired of fighting. Our chiefs are killed. Looking Glass is dead. Toohoolhoolzote is dead. The old men are all dead.

It is the young men who say yes and no. He who led on the young men is dead. It is cold and we have no blankets. The little children are freezing to death.

My people, some of them, have run away to the hills, and have no blankets, no food; no one knows where they are — perhaps freezing to death.

I want to have time to look for my children and see how many I can find. Maybe I shall find them among the dead.

Hear me, my chiefs. I am tired; my heart is sick and sad.

From where the sun now stands, I will fight no more forever.

Chief Joseph *Inmutooyahlatlat*

NEZ PERCÉ *Tsutpeli*

Chief Joseph made his speech of surrender to General Nelson Miles on October 5, 1877. Toohoolhoolzote was the Dreamer priest of Chief Joseph's band; Looking Glass was a fellow chief. Joseph died in 1904 on the Coleville Reservation, Washington.

William Henry Jackson *Looking Glass mounted on a painted war pony* Nez Percé 1871. Looking Glass was Joseph's principal war chief on his epic flight toward Canada and freedom in the summer and fall of 1877. He was killed the day before Chief Joseph made this speech of surrender.

THE GHOST DANCE

My children, when at first I liked the whites,
My children, when at first I liked the whites,
I gave them fruits,
I gave them fruits.

Father, have pity on me,
Father, have pity on me;
I am crying for thirst,
I am crying for thirst;
All is gone — I have nothing to eat,
All is gone — I have nothing to eat.

Father, the morning star!
Father, the morning star!
Look on us, we have danced until daylight,
Look on us, we have danced until daylight.
Take pity on us — Hi'i'i'!
Take pity on us — Hi'i'i'!

Ghost Dance songs

ARAPAHO *Inuna-ina*

The first of these three songs was composed by Nawat or Left Hand, chief of the southern Arapaho. The Ghost Dance religion was founded by the Paiute prophet Wovoka, who taught that, through dancing, the world would be renewed and the dead brought back to life. He said, "I went up to heaven and saw God and all the people who had died a long time ago. God told me to come back and tell my people they must be good and love one another, and not fight, or steal, or lie. He gave me this dance to give to my people." This peaceful doctrine (which echoed that of earlier prophets such as Smohalla) spread like wildfire through the Indian nations. It was seen as a threat by the whites, and led to the tragic massacre at Wounded Knee on December 29, 1890.

James Mooney *Arapaho Ghost Dancers — "Inspiration"* Arapaho 1890–1

George Trager *The battlefield of Wounded Knee*
Miniconjou Sioux 1891. Several
photographers recorded the terrible
scene at Wounded Knee, where
the dead lay frozen and unburied
for days. Another can be seen in
the foreground of this picture.

WHEN I LOOK BACK

When I look back now from this high hill of my old age, I can still see the butchered women and children lying heaped and scattered all along the crooked gulch as plain as when I saw them with eyes still young. And I can see that something else died there in the bloody mud, and was buried in the blizzard. A people's dream died there. It was a beautiful dream.

And I, to whom so great a vision was given in my youth — you see me now a pitiful old man who has done nothing, for the nation's hoop is broken and scattered. There is no center any longer, and the sacred tree is dead.

Black Elk *Hehaka Sapa*

OGLALA SIOUX Lakota

Black Elk is speaking of the Wounded Knee massacre of 1890, in which nearly 300 unarmed men, women, and children were slaughtered by soldiers of the Seventh U. S. Cavalry. Black Elk was an eye-witness.

Anonymous *Wovoka, prophet of the Ghost Dance* Paiute 1926

MY HEART IS A STONE

My heart is a stone: heavy with sadness for my people;
cold with the knowledge that no treaty will keep
whites out of our lands; hard with the determination
to resist as long as I live and breathe. Now we are
weak and many of our people are afraid. But hear me:
a single twig breaks, but the bundle of twigs is strong.
Someday I will embrace our brother tribes and draw
them into a bundle and together we will win our
country back from the whites.

Tecumseh

SHAWNEE

Spoken after the signing of the
Greenville treaty, ceding Shawnee
lands for worthless promises, in
August 1795. Tecumseh, who refused
to attend the treaty talks, succeeded
in uniting many midwestern and
southern tribes under his leadership
but died in battle in 1813.

Alexander Gardner *White Hawk, wife of
Big Foot* Miniconjou Sioux 1872. This
photograph was taken on a visit to
Washington, on which Big Foot, *Si
Tanka*, and his wife accompanied Chief
Red Cloud. It was Big Foot's band
that was attacked and massacred
at Wounded Knee. Both Big Foot
and White Hawk died.

CLEAR THE WAY

Clear the way
in a sacred manner
I come
the earth
is mine
hence
in a sacred manner
I come
clear the way
in a sacred manner
I come

Bear Eagle *Mato-wanbli*

TETON SIOUX *Lakota*

Bear Eagle learned this song from
Little Buffalo, *Tatanka-cikala.*

Lee Marmon *Laguna Eagle Dancers* Laguna 1949

FROM CHILDHOOD

From childhood I was consciously trained to be a man;
that was, after all, the basic thing; but after this I was
trained to be a warrior and a hunter, and not to care
for money or possessions, but to be in the broadest
sense a public servant. After arriving at a reverent
sense of the pervading presence of the Spirit and
Giver of Life, and a deep consciousness of the
brotherhood of man, the first thing for me to
accomplish was to adapt myself perfectly to natural
things — in other words, to harmonize myself with
nature. To this end I was made to build a body both
symmetrical and enduring — a house for the soul to live
in — a sturdy house, defying the elements. I must have
faith and patience; I must learn self-control and be
able to maintain silence. I must do with as little as
possible and start with nothing most of the time,
because a true Indian always shares whatever he may
possess.

Charles A. Eastman *Ohiyesa*

WAHPETON SIOUX *Lakota*

Eastman was brought up as a traditional
Sioux until the age of 15, when his
father sent him to school. He obtained
a degree in medicine from Boston
University and served as a
government doctor at the Pine Ridge
Agency, South Dakota, where he
treated the injured from the massacre
at Wounded Knee.

I SHALL NEVER DIE

My friend, I am old, but I shall never die. I shall
always live in my children, and children's children.

New Corn

POTAWATOMI

New Corn was speaking at the
signature of the Greenville peace
treaty in 1795.

The Miles Brothers *Two Siwash babies* Siwash 1902

WHEN A CHILD

When a child my mother taught me the legends of our people; taught me of the sun and sky, the moon and stars, the clouds and storms. She also taught me to kneel and pray to Usen for strength, health, wisdom, and protection. We never prayed against any person, but if we had aught against any individual we ourselves took vengeance. We were taught that Usen does not care for the petty quarrels of men.

My father had often told me of the brave deeds of our warriors, of the pleasures of the chase, and the glories of the warpath.

With my brothers and sisters I played about my father's home. Sometimes we played at hide-and-seek among the rocks and pines; sometimes we loitered in the shade of the cottonwood trees or sought the shudock [a kind of wild cherry] while our parents worked in the field. Sometimes we played that we were warriors. We would practice stealing upon some object that represented an enemy, and in our childish imitation often perform the feats of war. Sometimes we would hide away from our mother to see if she could find us, and often when thus concealed go to sleep and perhaps remain hidden for many hours.

Geronimo *Goyathlay*

CHIRICAHUA APACHE *Inde*

Camillus S. Fly *Geronimo (left, on horseback) and Naiche (in hat)* Chiricahua Apache 1886. The man standing to the left carrying a child is Geronimo's son.

Geronimo, born in 1829, was the most famous of Apache war chiefs. He died in 1909, having been a prisoner of war since 1886. Usen is the creator god of the Apache.

I LIKE TO LAUGH

That was a happy time on a happy world. There was always fat meat and glad singing. And yet, of course, there were many things that did not make us laugh when they happened, even though we laugh at them now. Looking back at things that frightened me when a girl I often laugh, alone. I like to laugh. I always did. Our hearts stay young if we let them.

Pretty-Shield

CROW *Absaroke*

Pretty-Shield told her life story to Frank B. Linderman. The book, published in 1932, carries her thumb-print as a mark of authenticity.

John Alvin Anderson *Katie Blue Thunder, aged 8* Brulé Sioux 1898

Sumner W. Matteson *Hopi girl at a window* Hopi 1901

TELLING THE TRUTH

I am ashamed before the earth;
I am ashamed before the heavens;
I am ashamed before the dawn;
I am ashamed before the evening twilight;
I am ashamed before the blue sky;
I am ashamed before the darkness;
I am ashamed before the sun;
I am ashamed before that standing within me
Which speaks with me.
Some of these things are always looking at me.
I am never out of sight.
Therefore I must tell the truth.
That is why I always tell the truth.
I hold my word tight to my breast.

Torlino

NAVAJO *Diné*

Torlino, a holy man of the Navajo,
spoke these words before reciting a
sacred myth to Washington
Matthews. Matthews explains "that
standing within me which speaks
with me" as "conscience."

Edward S. Curtis *Dancer representing the
god Zahadolzha* Navajo 1904

A CHANGE OF WORLDS

To us the ashes of our ancestors are sacred and their
resting place is hallowed ground. You wander far from
the graves of your ancestors and seemingly without
regret. Your religion was written on tables of stone by
the iron finger of your God so that you could not
forget. The red man could never comprehend nor
remember it. Our religion is the traditions of our
ancestors — the dreams of our old men, given them in
the solemn hours of night by the Great Spirit, and the
visions of our sachems [chiefs], and is written in the
hearts of our people.

Your dead cease to love you and the land of their
nativity as soon as they pass the portals of the tomb
and wander away beyond the stars. They are soon
forgotten and never return. Our dead never forget the
beautiful world that gave them being. They still love
its verdant valleys, its murmuring rivers, its
magnificent mountains, sequestered vales, and verdant-
lined lakes and bays, and ever yearn in tender, fond
affection over the lonely hearted living, and often
return from the Happy Hunting Ground to visit,
guide, console, and comfort them. . . .

Every part of this soil is sacred, in the estimation of
my people. Every hillside, every valley, every plain
and grove, has been hallowed by some sad or happy
event in days long vanished. Even the rocks, which
seem to be dumb and dead as they swelter in the sun
along the silent shore, thrill with memories of stirring
events connected with the lives of my people, and the
very dust upon which you now stand responds more

lovingly to their footsteps than to yours, because it is
rich with the dust of our ancestors and our bare feet
are conscious of the sympathetic touch. . . .

And when the last red man shall have perished, and
the memory of my tribe shall have become a myth
among the white man, these shores will swarm with
the invisible dead of my tribe, and when your
children's children think themselves alone in the field,
the store, the shop, upon the highway, or in the
silence of the pathless woods, they will not be alone.
In all the earth there is no place dedicated to solitude.
At night when the streets of your cities and villages
are silent and you think them deserted, they will
throng with the returning hosts that once filled them
and still love this beautiful land. The white man will
never be alone.

Let him be just and deal kindly with my people, for
the dead are not powerless. Dead — I say? There is no
death. Only a change of worlds.

Chief Seattle *Siahl*

SUQUAMISH/DUWAMISH *Salishan*

Chief Seattle (1786–1866) was
speaking in 1855 to Governor Isaac
Stevens, at the signing of the treaty
that surrendered the land where the
city of Seattle now stands.

Edward S. Curtis *Kickisomlo,*
known as Princess Angeline,
daughter of Chief Seattle
Suquamish/Duwamish 1899

THE END OF THE WORLD

Our people were made by the stars. When the time comes for all things to end, our people will turn into small stars and will fly to the South Star, where they belong. When the time comes for the ending of the world, the stars will again fall to the earth. They will mix among the people, for it will be a message to the people to get ready to be turned into stars.

Young Bull

PITAHAUERAT PAWNEE

Young Bull was described in 1906 as "the leading medicine-man among the Pitahauerat."

Edward S. Curtis *Arikara medicine ceremony — the ducks* Arikara 1908

John Alvin Anderson *Fool Bull* Brulé Sioux 1900

PRAYER FOR AMERICA

In the presence of this house, Grandfather, Wakan Tanka,
and from the direction where the sun sets,
and from the direction of cleansing power,
and from the direction of the rising sun,
and from the direction of the middle of the day,
Grandfather, Wakan Tanka,
Grandmother, the Earth who hears everything,
Grandmother, because you are woman, for this reason
    you are kind,
I come to you this day.

To tell you to love the red men, and watch over them,
and give these young men the understanding
because, Grandmother, from you come the good things,
good things that are beyond our eyes to see have been
    blessed in our midst,
for this reason I make my supplications known to you
    again.

On this day, on this great island, Grandfather,
upon which I stand, I make this prayer to you,
for those of us who are in this house.

Give us a blessing so that our words and actions
    be one in unity,
and that we be able to listen to each other,
in so doing, we shall with good heart walk
    hand in hand to face the future.

This is what I want for all of us,
for this reason, Grandfather and Grandmother,
    I make this thanksgiving prayer.

You give me this sacred pipe with which I pray
    to say thank you.
So be it.

In the presence of the outside, we are thankful
    for many blessings.
I make my prayer for all people, the children,
    the women, and the men.
I pray that no harm will come to them,
and that on the great island, there be no war,
that there be no ill feelings among us.
From this day on may we walk hand in hand.
So be it.

Frank Fools Crow

OGLALA SIOUX *Lakota*

On September 5, 1975, Fools Crow
became the first Native American
holy man to lead the opening prayer
for a session of the United States
Senate. These were his words.

Frank Richards *Rene Highway, a Cree dancer* Cree 1979

TEXT SOURCES

Grateful acknowledgment is made to the following sources and copyright holders. Every effort has been made to trace the owners of copyright, and we apologize for any omissions.

American State Papers. *Indian Affairs* vol. 1. Washington: Gales and Seaton, 1832. "I shall never die." **Bagley, Clarence B.** "Chief Seattle and Angeline." *Washington Historical Quarterly* vol. 22, no. 4, 1931. "A change of worlds." **Barrett, S. W.** *Geronimo: His Own Story*. New York: Duffield & Co., 1906. "When a child." **Black Hawk**. *Life of Ma-ka-tai-me-she-kia-kiak or Black Hawk*. Boston: Russell, Odiorne & Metcalf, 1834. "Land cannot be sold." **Brown, Joseph Epes**. *The Sacred Pipe: Black Elk's Account of the Seven Rites of the Oglala Sioux*. Norman: University of Oklahoma Press, 1953. "The earth." Copyright © 1953, 1989 by the University of Oklahoma Press. **Crow Dog, Leonard and Erdoes, Richard**. *Crow Dog: Four Generations of Sioux Medicine Men*. New York: HarperCollins, 1995. "A star whisper." Copyright © 1995 by Leonard Crow Dog and Richard Erdoes. **Densmore, Frances**. *Teton Sioux Music*. Washington: Smithsonian Institution Press, 1918. "In a sacred manner I live"; "The sun and the earth"; "A power greater than man"; "Clear the way." **Dorsey, George A.** *The Pawnee: Mythology (Part 1)*. Washington: Carnegie Institute of Washington, 1906. "The end of the world." **Drake, Samuel G.** *The Book of the Indians*. Boston: Antiquarian Bookstore, 1841. "Get a little farther"; "It is true"; "My heart is a stone." **Du Bois, Cora**. *Wintu Ethnography*. Berkeley: University of California Press, 1935. "The spirit of the earth." **Eastman, Charles A.** *The Soul of the Indian*. Boston: Houghton Mifflin, 1911. "The duty of prayer." *From the Deep Woods to Civilization*. Boston: Little, Brown, 1916. "From childhood." **Garrecht, Francis A.** "An Indian Chief." *The Washington Historical Quarterly* vol. 19, no. 3, 1928. "The Indian country." **Fire, John and Erdoes, Richard**. *Lame Deer: Seeker of Visions*. New York: Simon & Schuster, 1972. "When an Indian prays." Copyright © 1972 by John Fire/Lame Deer and Richard Erdoes. **Jacobs, Paul and Landau, Saul**. *To Serve the Devil* vol. 1. New York: Vintage Books, 1971. "The spring." **Jones, Rev. Peter**. *History of the Ojebway Indians*. London: A. W. Bennett, 1861. "I do not see any good." **Joseph, Chief**. "An Indian's View of Indian Affairs." *The North American Review* vol. 78, 1879. "This I believe"; "Words do not pay." **Linderman, Frank B.** *Red Mother*. New York: Harper, 1932. "I like to laugh." Copyright © 1932 by Frank B. Linderman, copyright renewed 1960. **Mails, Thomas E.** *Fools Crow*. Garden City, NY: Doubleday, 1979. "Prayer for America." Reprinted by permission of the University of Nebraska Press. Copyright © 1979 by Thomas E. Mails. **Matthews, Washington**. *Navaho Legends*. Boston: Houghton Mifflin, 1897. "Telling the truth." *Navaho Myths, Prayers, and Songs* (ed. Pliny Earle Goddard). Berkeley: University of Calfornia Press, 1907. "In beauty may I walk." **McCreight, M. I.** *Firewater and Forked Tongues: A Sioux Chief Interprets U. S. History*. Pasadena: Trail's End Publishing Co., Inc., 1947. "The tipi." **McLintock, Walter**. *The Old North Trail: Life, Legends and Religion of the Blackfoot Indians*. London: Macmillan & Co., 1910. "The sun god." **Miller, Lee**. *From the Heart: Voices of the American Indian*. New York: Alfred A. Knopf, 1995. "Land is more valuable than money." **Mooney, James**. *The Ghost Dance Religion and the Sioux Outbreak of 1890*. Washington: Smithsonian Institution Press, 1896. "You ask me to plow the ground!"; "Ghost dance songs." **Moquin, Wayne and Van Doren, Charles**. *Great Documents in American Indian History*. New York: Praeger Publishers, 1973. "I want peace." **Neihardt, John G.** *Black Elk Speaks*. New York: Morrow, 1932. "Behold this day"; "The great circle"; "When I look back." Reprinted by permission of the University of Nebraska Press. Copyright © 1932, 1959, 1972 by John G. Neihardt. Copyright © 1961 by the John G. Neihardt Trust. **O'Bryan, Aileen**. *The Diné: Origin Myths of the Navaho Indians*. Washington: Smithsonian Institution Press, 1955. "Looking into the future." **Red Cloud**. "Speech at Cooper Institute." New York *Tribune*, Jan. 16, 1870. "Look at me." **Smith, Captain John**. *Works*. Birmingham: The English Scholar's Library, 1884. "Peace and war." **Thatcher, B. B.** *Indian Biography*. New York: Harper & Brothers, 1845. "There was a time." **U.S. Congress House Executive Committee Documents**. *Report of the Commissioner for Indian Affairs*, 1870-1. "The true teacher." *Report of the U.S. Secretary of War*, 1877-8. "I will fight no more." **U.S. Senate Hearings of the Interior and Insular Affairs Committee**. *Problems of Electrical Power Production in the Southwest*, 1971. "The earth is our mother."

PICTURE SOURCES

Grateful acknowledgment is made to the following institutions and individuals.

Amon Carter Museum, Fort Worth, Texas 18, 25 (© 1981, Laura Gilpin Collection); **British Library** 2-3, 5, 10, 14, 21, 30, 33, 35, 36, 47, 63, 64, 82, 85, 87, 94-5 (shelfmark L. R. 298. a. 32); **Library of Congress** 17 (neg. 19725), 20 (neg. 2315), 77 (neg. 101194); **Lee Marmon** 74-5 (© 1949); **Milwaukee Public Museum** 81 (neg. 44,509); **Montana Historical Society** 55 (neg. 955-982); **Nebraska Historical Society** 44 (neg. A547-1), 70 (neg. W938-119-33), 80 (neg. A547-165A), 88 (neg.

INDEX OF SPEAKERS

INDEX OF INDIAN NATIONS

FURTHER READING

Brown, Dee. *Bury My Heart at Wounded Knee: An Indian History of the American West.* New York: Henry Holt, 1970.
Griffin-Pierce, Trudy. *The Encyclopaedia of Native America.* New York: Viking, 1995.
Hausman, Gerald. *Turtle Island Alphabet: A Lexicon of Native American Symbols and Culture.* New York: St. Martin's Press, 1992.
Josephy, Alvin M., Jr. *500 Nations: An Illustrated History of North American Indians.* New York: Alfred A. Knopf, 1994.
Krupat, Arnold. *Native American Autobiography: An Anthology.* Madison: The University of Wisconsin Press, 1994.
McLuhan, T. C. *Touch the Earth: A Self-Portrait of Indian Existence.* New York: Outerbridge and Dienstfrey, 1971.
Miller, Lee. *From the Heart: Voices of the American Indian.* New York: Alfred A. Knopf, 1995.
Moquin, Wayne, and Van Doren, Charles. *Great Documents in American Indian History.* New York: Da Capo Press, 1995.
Nabokov, Peter. *Native American Testimony: A Chronicle of Indian-White Relations from Prophecy to the Present, 1492– 1992.* New York: Viking, 1991.
Swanton, John R. *The Indian Tribes of North America.* Washington: Smithsonian Institution Press, 1952.

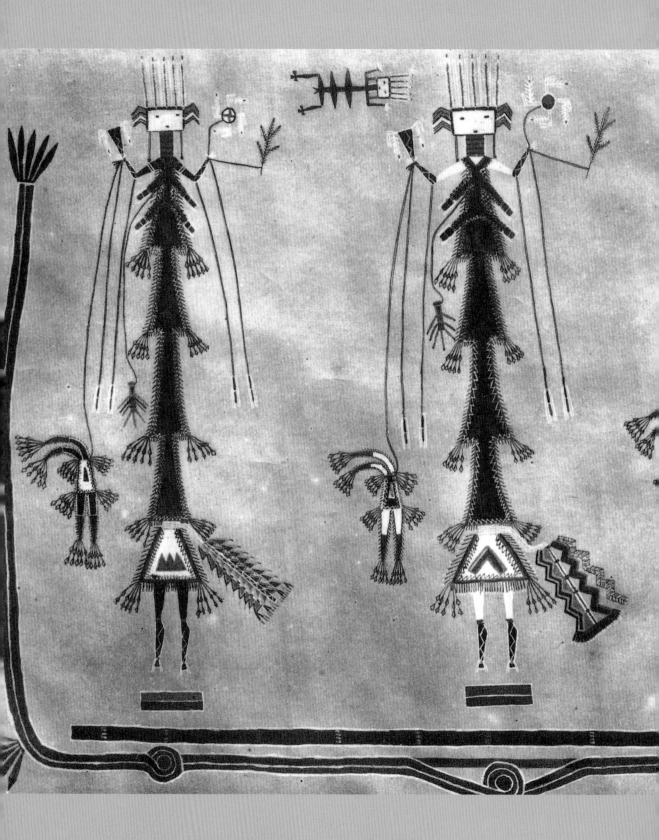

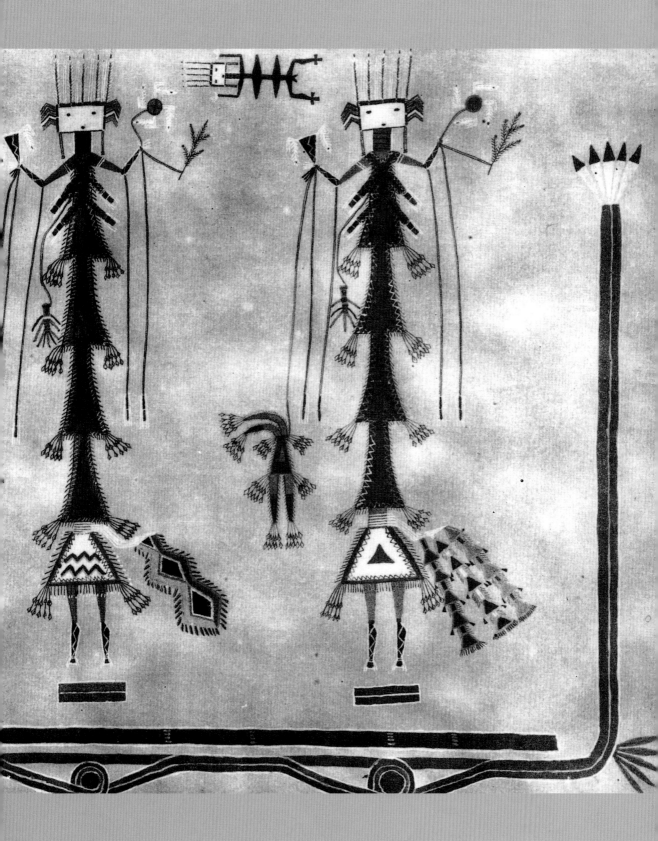